I Can Go to Church!

A Unique Guide for Kids

By Madeline Lindke & Dr. Rachel Youngblom
Illustrated by Jemimah Grove

Introduction

This book is written much like a social story that can be used as a tool to help a child by setting some common expectations for worship time. It does not instruct an institution or even a parent. It's a tool for practice whenever you attend church. The first side of each page expresses what your child might see in church; the second side provides a common behavioral expectation for that context.

Your child may need a break during church. As your child's caregiver, you know what that means for your child and can help with the appropriate response. Your child may never sit through a whole service. Celebrate little milestones as you use this book.

Worship services differ from church to church. That's why these pages are interchangeable. Put them in the order of your worship service. You'll find multiple song/hymn pages to place where songs come in the service. Store unused pages in the back.

After arranging the pages to fit your upcoming worship service, walk through the book with your child the day before—or even multiple times during the week before. Take the book to worship and walk the child through it again while the service is taking place.

Madeline Lindke is a mother of two, one of whom is on the autism spectrum. Sometimes during worship, she and her son pace and "regulate" in the back of their church in Illinois.

Dr. Rachel Youngblom is a school psychologist and trained in special education. She instructs future teachers at Martin Luther College in New Ulm, Minnesota.

Jemimah Grove is a freelance artist who lives with her husband and daughter in South Korea.

Thanks to WELS Special Ministries for the encouraging input and financial support.

And thanks to every parent and caregiver who works to make worship meaningful for children. May God bless your efforts to bring your child into a happy worship life with Christ Jesus our dear Savior!

"Happy are those you choose and bring near to settle within your walls. We are filled with the good things of your house, your holy temple!"
(Psalm 65:4)

All rights reserved. This publication may not be copied, photocopied, reproduced, translated, or converted to any electronic or machine-readable form in whole or in part, except for brief quotations, without prior written approval from the publisher.

Northwestern Publishing House
N16W23379 Stone Ridge Dr., Waukesha WI 53188-1108
www.nph.net
© 2025 Madeline Lindke and Rachel Youngblom
Published by Northwestern Publishing House 2025
Printed in China
ISBN 978-0-8100-3279-8

1601639
ISBN 978-0-8100-3279-8
9780810032798

On special days of the week, I go to church

with my family to learn about God.

I love to learn about him.

I see lots of people.

I can smile and wave or say "Hi" to them.

I Can Go to Church, published by Northwestern Publishing House, ©

If it gets too loud or too hot,

I can ask my family for help.

I can use my words or communication board.

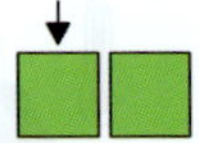

Before the service starts,

I can pick out my seat in church.

I can ask for help if my body needs to move.

I Can Go to Church, published by Northwestern Publishing House, ©

I see different lights or candles.

I smell different smells,

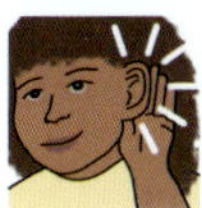

and I hear music.

Someone might be praying

so I need to be quiet and use my soft voice or

communication board if I need something.

I Can Go to Church, published by Northwestern Publishing House, ©

I hear people

using their voices to sing.

This is a special song to God.

Hymn • Song

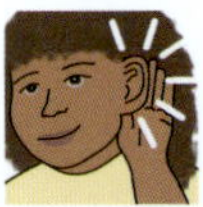

I can listen to the words and music.

I can sit and sing along too.

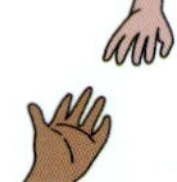

If it’s too loud, I can ask for help.

I Can Go to Church, published by Northwestern Publishing House, ©

We are welcomed to church, and sometimes

we say a special prayer to start the service.

We talk to God when we pray.

When it's time to pray,

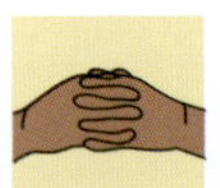

I can fold or raise my hands to God.

I can bow my head and close my eyes.

I can listen to the words of the prayer.

I Can Go to Church, published by Northwestern Publishing House, ©

We tell God

we are sorry for the bad things we do.

The bad things are called sins.

We all pray together.

It might be out loud or in our minds.

I can listen and join in.

I Can Go to Church, published by Northwestern Publishing House, ©

The best thing is that

God forgives all my sins because of Jesus!

Jesus died on the cross and took away my sins.

I can listen to the words of forgiveness.

I feel happy that God forgives me.

I Can Go to Church, published by Northwestern Publishing House, ©

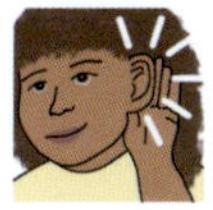

I listen to the Bible reading with my family.

Everyone needs to hear God's Word.

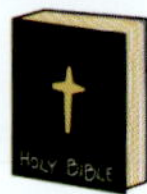

I can follow along in the Bible,

or I can sit quietly and listen.

I love to hear God's words.

I Can Go to Church, published by Northwestern Publishing House, ©

There is a special lesson

just for me and the other kids.

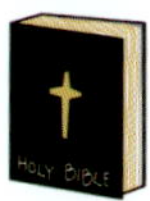

This helps me understand God's Word.

I can sit and listen with a quiet body.

I can focus on the person

teaching me about God.

I Can Go to Church, published by Northwestern Publishing House, ©

A speaker tells us a special message.

This message helps me

understand the Bible.

It’s important that I stay quiet

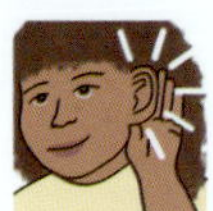

so everyone can hear. I can ask my family

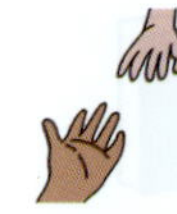

for help or a break if I need it.

I Can Go to Church, published by Northwestern Publishing House, ©

"We believe..."

Everyone says the creed.

This is when we say what we believe.

"I believe..."

I can say the creed with everyone.

I can say it out loud or in my head.

I Can Go to Church, published by Northwestern Publishing House, ©

"Great is your faithfulness, God. I love you!"

"Thank you, Lord, for loving me!"

"Father, forgive me for my sins. Help me not to be tempted."

We pray to God. We say "Thank you," and

we tell him we love him. We also pray

 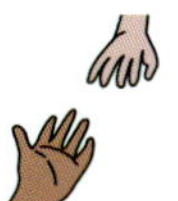

to say we are sorry and to ask for help.

When it's time to pray,

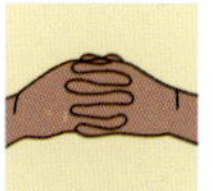

I can fold or raise my hands to God.

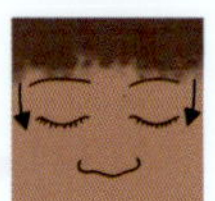

I can bow my head and close my eyes.

I can listen to the words of the prayer.

I Can Go to Church, published by Northwestern Publishing House, ©

"Our Father..."

We say the Lord's Prayer.

This is a prayer Jesus teaches us

in the Bible.

When it's time to pray,

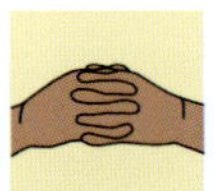 

I can fold or raise my hands to God.

I can bow my head and close my eyes.

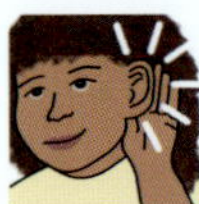

I can listen to the words of the Lord's Prayer.

I Can Go to Church, published by Northwestern Publishing House, ©

We thank God by giving him an offering.

We give our gifts to God

with love in our hearts.

I can put my offering

in the collection for God.

I love to thank God this way.

I Can Go to Church, published by Northwestern Publishing House, ©

Holy Communion is special bread and wine

people eat and drink at church.

It is an important gift of Jesus' body and blood,

a special way he says, "I forgive you!"

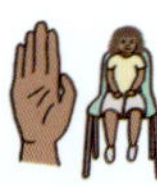 

I can be patient and listen.

This will help me understand

the big gift from Jesus.

I Can Go to Church, published by Northwestern Publishing House, ©

"The LORD bless you..."

We receive a final blessing.

This is how God promises to watch over us

and give us peace in the week to come.

"Amen!"

I can say or think "Amen"

at the end of the blessing.

I Can Go to Church, published by Northwestern Publishing House, ©

We hear announcements of

what will happen during the week at church.

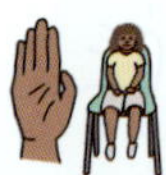

I can be patient and wait my turn

to leave church. I can wait with my family,

and I can follow instructions.

I Can Go to Church, published by Northwestern Publishing House, ©

Yay! I went to church!

I learned about God,

and I can do it again when I go to church next!

End of Church

Communication Board

Add your own in the blank spaces

I Can Go to Church, published by Northwestern Publishing House, ©

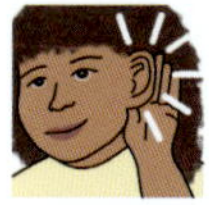

I hear people

using their voices to sing.

This is a special song to God.

Hymn • Song

I can listen to the words and music.

I can sit and sing along too.

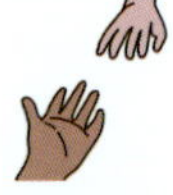

If it's too loud, I can ask for help.

Hymn • Song

I Can Go to Church, published by Northwestern Publishing House, ©

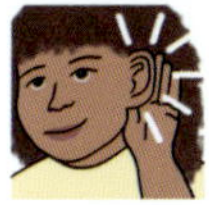

I hear people

using their voices to sing.

This is a special song to God.

Hymn • Song

I can listen to the words and music.

I can sit and sing along too.

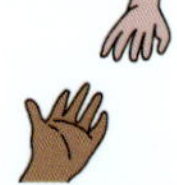

If it's too loud, I can ask for help.

I Can Go to Church, published by Northwestern Publishing House, ©

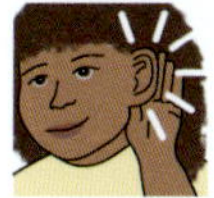

I hear people

using their voices to sing.

This is a special song to God.

Hymn • Song

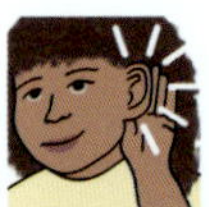

I can listen to the words and music.

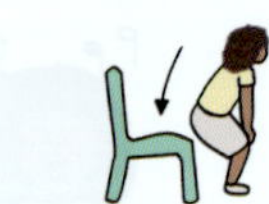 

I can sit and sing along too.

If it’s too loud, I can ask for help.

Hymn • Song

I Can Go to Church, published by Northwestern Publishing House, ©

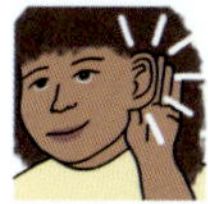

I hear people

using their voices to sing.

This is a special song to God.

Hymn • Song

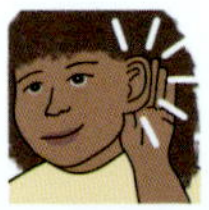

I can listen to the words and music.

I can sit and sing along too.

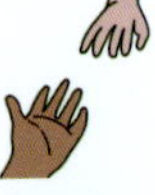

If it's too loud, I can ask for help.

Hymn • Song

I Can Go to Church, published by Northwestern Publishing House, ©

"Great is your faithfulness, God. I love you!"

"Thank you, Lord, for loving me!"

"Father, forgive me for my sins. Help me not to be tempted."

We pray to God. We say "Thank you," and

we tell him we love him. We also pray

 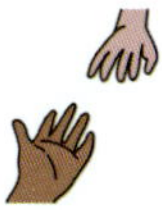

to say we are sorry and to ask for help.

When it's time to pray,

I can fold or raise my hands to God.

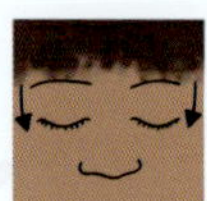

I can bow my head and close my eyes.

I can listen to the words of the prayer.

I Can Go to Church, published by Northwestern Publishing House, ©

I Can Go to Church!

Includes extra pages for **CUSTOMIZING**

I Can Go to Church!

"I want my child to be part of church, but sometimes it's hard for him to stay engaged!"

Children with shorter attention spans or special needs can find it challenging and even overwhelming to participate in worship.

I Can Go to Church! is a customizable picture book, with pages easily rearranged to match the specific flow of your church's worship service. Designed to help each child participate in church in a way that works individually, it explains every part of the worship service with easy words and colorful images. The book also includes helpful steps to follow so your child knows what she or he can do next, and there's even a communication board for quietly sharing feelings and needs during the service.

Your child may not be able to sit through an entire service—and that's perfectly okay. *I Can Go to Church!* is designed to help take small, manageable steps toward participation. Celebrate each milestone as your child grows, learns, and finds joy in worship!

Meet the Authors

Madeline Lindke is a mother of two, one of whom is on the autism spectrum.

Dr. Rachel Youngblom is a college professor in special education and trains future teachers.

1601639
ISBN 978-0-8100-3279-8
9780810032798